And one day I heard it.

It was loud.

It was clear.

It was defiant.

It was me.

Journal Entry
October 17, 2014

I often find myself sitting here on the floor of this closet. I guess this has become my safe zone, my secret space I run to when the noise of this life becomes too much.

I should be happy right? I am a wife. I am a mother. I have a great house. I have a nice car. I have a great job, I feel as if I have all my boxes checked. I mean, after everything I have been through, I deserve to have this life I have created. I should be happy. But………

I don't think anyone even notices that I always feel stuck, trapped, and stagnant. That I am struggling to find my place. That I am drowning in the life I have created and there are days that I can't even recognize my own voice. Everything around me is falling apart. I am failing.

I don't think anyone even notices that I am falling back into old habits. It is crazy how something so small can drag you back to the memories of a life that you have worked so hard to forget. Just that quick I have been snapped back to that little girl dying for someone to rescue her. That little girl that seemed to struggle forever with "Why don't they…"

I don't think anyone really knows how to find your voice when you were never sure of what it sounded like from the beginning. My mind swarms with the thoughts of how in the hell did I get here. Now I am confronted by memories that I would prefer to just forget because I refuse to give them credit for where I am. When, in reality, I have been shaped by the struggle of trying to figure out why. Why don't they love me? Why can't they support me? Why do they constantly treat me different? Why is what I do never good enough. Why didn't they ever want me? How do you replace family? These are the people that are supposed to love you right?

I used to dream of someone, anyone coming to rescue me. But no one ever came. Feelings of inadequacy turned into a secret longing for acceptance, which then turned into hate, have now blossomed into a serious I don't give a, you know. Yet now it seems that no matter how far I try to run, I always end up right back here where I started.

I don't think anyone knows that there are days I feel my life is a complete lie. Picture perfect smiles that lead to loneliness behind closed doors. I should be happy. After everything I have been through I deserve this. I want this. Why doesn't this life want me back? Life is a funny thing. It gives you exactly what you think you want just to help you learn exactly what it is you really need. My heart is broken. Every day I struggle with the failure of not knowing and not understanding how to fix this; how to fix us. But I am not brave enough to just drop it all and walk away.

I don't think anyone really knows how much I struggled today. You force me to unpack the parts of me I have neatly tucked away, and today my insecurities are unraveling. I hate how you make me feel. I hate the places you take me back to. Who is this person? Who am I if I am no longer a wife? Who am I if I no longer have all the answers? Who am I without this life? How do you pick up the pieces when you are losing grip on everything you use to define your worth?

I don't think anyone notices how much of yourself you must confront before you can heal and move forward. What they never tell you is that healing hurts before it starts to get better, and it never shows up in the form you would expect it to. I have found that sometimes healing looks like forgiving even when people won't acknowledge how much they have affected you. Sometimes healing looks like walking away and coming to terms with the fact that there are times you must let go of what you want to get what it is you need. Sometimes, healing looks like sitting in your closet in the dark and silencing the world around you so that your voice can be heard.

UNBECOMING EVERYTHING

Latisha M. Bickham

It's in those quiet still moments that we find the answers we are looking for

It's ok not to be ok. It's ok to regroup. It's ok to refocus. It's ok to rebrand. It's ok to re-engage.

Are you ready to get to know yourself a little better? Unbecoming Everything is an introspective journey of self-exploration that is compiled of a series of questions and activities that will steer you through the acceptance and acknowledgement phase of self-discovery to the challenge of developing actionable steps that will align who you are now with where you envision yourself in the future. As you embark on your journey of Unbecoming Everything you will begin to:

- Uncover who you are outside of life's expectations

- Address your hidden wants and needs without the input of outside influences

- Get honest with yourself about where you are in life now

- Identify changes in your life that you may not have been aware you needed

- Challenge yourself to move forward toward your goals

Each phase is an invitation through the journey of self-exploration:

Phase 1: Beyond the Expectations: Restart. Reset. Refocus.
Phase 2: Discover. Empower. Become: What do you want?
Phase 3: Evolve or Repeat: Where are you now?
Phase 4: I'm D.O.P.E: What will you do?
Phase 5: Note to Self: Living Brings Lessons

Your journey of Unbecoming Everything is only one page away.

We live in a society where people are trying to discover who they are while drowning in a sea of expectations.

Beyond the Expectations: Restart. Reset. Refocus.

Who is this person? A Mirrored Reflection.

Somehow, somewhere, something happened, and I just didn't know who I was anymore. It's like I woke up and found myself just stuck:

- Feeling stagnant
- Struggling to find my place
- Dealing with failure and setbacks
- Shattered dreams
- Losing my voice
- Dealing with depression and anxiety
- Dealing with self-doubt
- Dealing with fear
- Dealing with self-limiting behaviors

Struggling to answer the question who am I, if I am no longer……

Becoming who I wanted to be, who I was meant to be was a voyage of acceptance. All the pieces I thought were missing the parts I needed to take control of my life were already there. Everything I needed to overcome those obstacles and accomplish those goals. Everything that makes me…..ME was already there just waiting to be discovered.

Exploration Activities

You can choose one of the following activities or you can complete them all.

- Look in the mirror and say "I love you just the way you are with no expectations."

- Start a gratitude list, add one thing to the list each morning

- Commit to a 24 hr Social Media Detox

I LIKE ME BETTER

I AM......

Define who you are without using any of the following:

- Name
- Job Title/Professional Titles
- Relationship Titles
- Things you like to do
- Things you do for others

Once you are done take a moment and reflect on this exercise.

How was it for you?

When you take away all the titles and expectations that life comes with, do you recognize what is left over?

In what ways do you try and define yourself through the expectations of others or personal accomplishments?

Phase 1: Beyond the Expectations: Restart. Reset. Refocus.

Reflect on how your life has been up to this point.

What does success look like for you?

What are some challenges you have faced that you would have never thought you'd have the strength to overcome?

Phase 1: Beyond the Expectations: Restart. Reset. Refocus.

The mess ups, the failures, and the hurts of your past do not have to follow you into your new beginning.

Take a moment and think about what you feel are your biggest regrets?

What steps can you take to make amends and forgive yourself so you can begin healing?

Phase 1: Beyond the Expectations: Restart. Reset. Refocus.

The only thing that is definite in life is that one day it must come to an end.

Take a moment and reflect on where you are in life now. Think about all your failures, successes, goals, regrets, dreams.

Today you learned that the next Friday would ultimately be your last.

Explore how this makes you feel.

How will you be remembered? How can you use this as motivation to accomplish your goals?

Phase 1: Beyond the Expectations: Restart. Reset. Refocus.

I'm afraid people wouldn't
love or accept me if they knew

_____.

How does this hold you back from being
your most authentic self?

The journey is not meant to be comfortable

Take a moment to reflect on
toxic behaviors you struggle with.

How do they drain your energy?

What can you do to remove these things
from your life or set boundaries that
protect you from their negative effects?

Phase 1: Beyond the Expectations: Restart. Reset. Refocus.

Way to commit!

Take a moment and think about
how the first phase of this journey
has been so far.

Have you enjoyed it? Or was it difficult?

What have you learned about
 yourself so far?

Phase 1: Beyond the Expectations: Restart. Reset. Refocus.

BE BOLD.
Take Risks.

Exceed Your Expectations.

Believe in YOUR power.

Focus on becoming your best self
& NEVER look back.

Discover• Empower• Become
What do you want? A Mirrored Reflection.

> Starting Over
> Self Accountability
> Learning to trust the process
> # What do your goals look like?
> Creating more balance
> Self Care
> ESTABLISHING PRIORITIES
> Discovering your passion

Make your vision so clear that the fear becomes irrelevant.

Exploration Activities

You can choose one of the following activities or you can complete them all.

- Create a 'stop doing this' list

- This week focus on being intentional with your time and energy

- Become more aware of what changes your self-talk

The process isn't
always about
figuring out how to
reinvent the wheel.

It's about finding ways to dedicate
YOUR creativity,
YOUR energy,
and YOUR experience
in order to make an
idea YOUR own.

Yeah anyone can do it,
but no one will ever do it like you.

Trying to complete your goals all at once can cause you to become discouraged, especially if they take too long to complete or they do not go exactly how you planned.

Instead, shift your focus to creating smaller more attainable goals that will get you closer to your result each day.

What is a goal that you put off because you got discouraged along the way? Are you ready to recommit to that goal?

If so, try the SUCCESS format to help reach your desired results.

(S)elect a dream. Envision what you want and clarify why this is important to you.

(U)se your dream to set goals. Define what you want to achieve.

(C)reate a plan. Be specific on what how you will get there. How will you reward yourself for completing each task?

(C)onsider your resources. Is everything you need to get the job done readily available to you?

(E)nhance your skills and abilities. Make sure you have access to all the tools, support, and knowledge needed to get the job done.

(S)pend time wisely. Get organized. Get Motivated. Pay attention to your self-talk.

(S)tart.

Phase 2: Discover. Empower. Become: What do you want?

Take a moment and think about how
you currently go about making
decisions.

Do you allow other people's expectations, fears, and what if's
influence how you make your
decisions?

Reflect on how this has hindered or
stopped you from being able to move
forward with pursuing your own wishes and dreams.

Today you're outlining a new
three-part book series that will be based on your life.

The last book focuses on the end of your life?
How do you want the story to end?

What changes would you have to make in life now
for the story to end the way you'd like?

Walking in your purpose is a choice.

Life is just waiting for you to make it.

What is something you have always wanted to do but you have found yourself so worried about not being able to control the outcome that you haven't even tried?

What are some steps you could implement to let go of the "what if" worries?

Today you received some great news.

That project you finished last week hit big and because of this you've been given a livable income for the rest of your life.

You're not millionaire rich, but you no longer must work either.

You're comfortable.

What would you focus on now? What would you do with all your free time?

Sometimes the fear doesn't go away.

Do It Afraid!

Imagine you were granted the opportunity to
go back in time to age of 18.

You are allowed to leave a letter for your 18 year-old self.

What advice would you share?

What would you try to change?

Complete this thought

I CAN BE	AND STILL BE
•	•
•	•
•	•
•	•

What can you do differently within the next 90 days to make this a reality?

Is there anything you would have to sacrifice to make this a reality?

Are you willing to make this sacrifice?

Phase 2: Discover. Empower. Become: What do you want?

The scars, bumps, and bruises of life's journey are proof you have what it takes to survive.

Evolve or Repeat
Where are you now? A Mirrored Reflection.

You are not limited to what you have been through.

You are not limited to who or what other people expect you to be.

You are whatever it is YOU are determined to become.

But... it starts with telling the truth to yourself first.

It is easy to say I'm going to change. The hard part is forcing yourself to pull back the curtain and take a good inventory of all the past hurts, fears, and insecurities that have you stuck in the first place.

We tend to try and bury the ugliness of our past not realizing that you will never align with your vision of the future if you don't take the time to understand how your past effects your present.

So instead of holding onto past hurts, setbacks, and fears allowing them to control your future, it is time adjust your view. Focus on the strength you had to overcome.

Exploration Activities

You can choose one of the following activities or you can complete them all.

- Write 3 affirmations that remind you of your value. Commit to reciting them everyday

- Don't eat lunch at a desk for a week

- Get dressed up and take yourself out for a date

Stop letting people tell you what you can't do.

I dare you to trust your voice.

Mind Dump

Write down everything that is going through your mind right now.

It doesn't matter how trivial you think it is. Taking the time to identify issues, fears and insecurities is the first step to overcoming them.

It's time to take your power back.

Do you have unfinished business?

Are you holding on to something that would
make your life so much easier if you were to just let it go?

What inner work needs to be done to heal this?

What are some steps you can take to begin bringing this to resolution?

What are some self-limiting thoughts or toxic behaviors you have that negatively affect your life?

Do you intentionally sabotage yourself?

Do you remember where or when these behaviors started?

What are some positive actions you can implement to counterbalance these behaviors?

Phase 3: Evolve or Repeat: Where are you now?

Think about the people you currently align yourself with (family, friends, associates, etc).

What kinds of people are you investing in?

Do you feel supported?
What are they pushing you to become?

How do you feel about this?

Think about what you consider to be the most important things people should know about you.

Write a 6-word narrative of how you would like to be remembered.

How do these words reflect what is most important to you?

List 3 decisions or changes you are currently struggling with in your life right now.

If you had 15 days to change or get rid of them, how would you do it?

Where would you start?

What does your inner critic say to you?

How does this stop you from moving forward?

What can you do to change this voice?

Phase 3: Evolve or Repeat: Where are you now?

Of course it's going to be hard.

But it's not impossible.

I'm D.O.P.E: Defying Other People's Expectations.
What will you do? A Mirrored Reflection.

Stop living to prove THEM wrong.

I've wasted a lot of time trying to prove THEM wrong.

Constantly telling myself I'm doing this because THEY don't think I can.

Convincing myself that I need to stay where I am because THEY didn't think I could get here.

Just stuck drowning in a life that I didn't want because it didn't matter if my happiness got sacrificed.

I just needed to show THEM.

It's time to stop trying to prove THEM wrong and focus on defining the path that is meant for you.

Give yourself permission to step into the life that is meant for you.

Exploration Activities

You can choose one of the following activities or you can complete them all.

- Pick something new to learn this week

- Take an hour and begin working on something you've been putting off

- Take a day and dedicate it to yourself

What type of gifts do you feel you possess that are uniquely yours to share with others?

In what ways do you nurture these gifts?

Think about a time you used your gifts to help someone else with a struggle or an obstacle they were facing.

How did this make you feel?

How can you use this experience to determine what you'd like to explore in the next chapter of your life?

Phase 4: I'm D.O.P.E: What will you do?

Most companies and organizations use mission statements as a way to summarize their values, purpose, and goals.

Are you aware of your mission?

Write a mission statement for yourself.

Write a letter accepting an apology you may not receive.

_____
_____
_____
_____
_____
_____
_____
_____
_____
_____
_____

Phase 4: I'm D.O.P.E: What will you do?

Take a moment to reflect on the things that matter to you the most.

Did you make the list?

How far did you get before you considered yourself? How does this make you feel?

What can you do to make yourself more of a priority in your life?

Phase 4: I'm D.O.P.E: What will you do?

Taking up a new hobby, trying a new restaurant…

When was the last time you had an experience that was just for you?

How much personal time are you willing to dedicate to yourself each week?

How can you hold yourself accountable for accomplishing this?

Phase 4: I'm D.O.P.E: What will you do?

What life lesson did you learn the hard way?

How can you use this experience as you
work to accomplish your goals?

You can't win if you *NEVER* start.

You can't learn if you *NEVER* start.

You will never know what you are capable of if you *NEVER* start.

So take the risk, you're definitely worth it.

NOTE TO SELF....
Living brings lessons. A Mirrored Reflection.

---

1. Trust your gut. If it feels wrong, don't do it.

2. No is an answer. Sometimes further explanation is not needed or deserved.

3. Don't get so wrapped up in the bigger picture that you forget to celebrate the mini milestones.

4. Never be afraid to experience life.

5. There is enough room in there to love yourself and others without having to sacrifice or choose.

6. The only person obligated to support you is YOU.

7. When you are more focused on competing or comparing yourself to others, you miss out on the opportunities to just be yourself.

NOTE TO SELF....
Living brings lessons. A Mirrored Reflection.

---

8. Write it down. There is nothing more motivating than having your goals staring back at you.

9. Obsessing over another person's journey does nothing productive for your own.

10. Comfort can paralyze you.

11. You can't just live in hope every day, you need to take action.

12. Stepping into your purpose requires sacrifice, but the moment where you feel you've lost everything is when you find YOU.

13. It's not the idea of change that makes you afraid. It's the fear of not being able to control what happens next.

14. Don't waste your energy trying to hold on to something that you know isn't meant for you.

Exploration Activities

You can choose one of the following activities or you can complete them all.

- Dedicate to 15 mins of silence each day for a week

- Work on not explaining your choices for a week let your No mean No

- Make it a celebration. Focus on everything that goes right this week

Take a moment a write out what you would
consider to be your most important
needs and desires? Choose 5

Does your present life support or fulfill these?

If not, how can you change or adjust
to better align yourself to meet these
needs?

Complete this letter.

Dear Self,

I am sorry that _____.

I love you because _____.

I want you to know that _____.

When was the last time you took a good
look at your self in the mirror and pointed
out everything you liked about what it is you see?

Create a list of your five favorite strengths.

Sometimes life will shake everything up to show you that you are worth more than you're settling for

DISCOVER·EMPOWER·BECOME

How will you challenge yourself to keep moving forward?

1. ENVISION

My _____ day Bold Vision is to: _____

_____

_____

_____

_____

_____

2. ENABLE

I need this change because: _____

_____

_____

_____

_____

3. ENGAGE

This is where I am starting: _____

_____

_____

_____

_____

This is how I will get there:
(Make sure you refer back to the Goal SUCCESS format)

Goal 1:	Goal 2:	Goal 3:	Goal 4:	Goal 5:

4. ENERGIZE

If I get discouraged, I will remind myself that:

_____
_____
_____
_____

As I complete each goal, I will reward myself by:

_____
_____
_____
_____

5. EXECUTE

I will set this plan in motion by: ____/____/____

Journal Entry
December 12, 2015

I spent years searching for the sound of my voice.
The sound it makes when I am happy.
The blare of disappointment and anger.
The tone it takes when I am sad.
The descent of the scales when I am tired and in need of a break.

I spent years searching for the sound of my voice.
The pitch it takes when I am confident in my approach.
The frequency of my words when I get excited.
The bass that comes with knowing what it is I want, and not being afraid to say it.

I spent years searching for the sound of my voice.
The voice that is unmovable.
The voice that is unshakable.
The voice that is louder than the world around me.

I spent years searching for the sound of my voice.
Then one day, in the middle of all the chaos and confusion surrounding me, I heard something.
It was loud.
It was clear.
It was defiant.

It was me.

Copyright © 2019 Latisha M. Bickham
All rights reserved. This book or any portion thereof may not be reproduced or used in any manner whatsoever without the express written permission of the publisher except for the use of brief quotations in a book review or scholarly journal.
First Printing: 2019
ISBN 978-0-578-22182-3

I'Jale Publishing Co LLC
2431 Manhattan Blvd.
Suite C
Harvey, La. 70058
www.ijalepublishing.com

www.ingramcontent.com/pod-product-compliance
Lightning Source LLC
Chambersburg PA
CBHW020810160426
43192CB00006B/511